THE ROOMMATE BOOK

THE ROOMMATE BOOK

SHARING LIVES & SLAPPING FIVES

BECKY SIMPSON

Andrews McMeel Publishing®

a division of Andrews McMeel Universal

Other books by Becky Simpson

I'd Rather Be Short

To all of my roommates.

You know who you are.

CONTENTS

INTRODUCTION

I was sitting at my desk working on an illustration project when I had the idea to write a book about roommates. My then roommate, Bekah, had said something funny. Or maybe she did something funny. Or maybe I just remembered something that we saw that was funny. I don't recall the details of that moment, but I do remember feeling like the idea came out of nowhere.

But it didn't come out of nowhere. The inspiration really wasn't that single lightning rod moment; it was an eight-year catalog of memories with Bekah and some of the other best roommates around.

Allow me to explain.

There's this song by Dead Man's Bones (Ryan Gosling's band) called "Pa Pa Power."

Bekah and I discovered it a couple of years ago, well after its release in 2009. We were late bloomers, even when it came to music; but we didn't care because *we loved that song.*

Somewhere along the way, a tradition was born. Every time "Pa Pa Power" was played, we dropped whatever we were doing to lunge-dance-exercise for the duration of the song. We called this "lancing." It was the only apartment rule to which we seriously abided. In fact, sometimes one of us would play it at five a.m. and force the other to jump out of bed and engage in four minutes of "hardcore lancing." Because it was a serious tradition, we had to do it. No questions asked. Side note: This exercise not only builds character, but also an incredible ability to get quite low on the dance floor (whether it be *Matrix* or Sally O'Malley style). For this, I am forever grateful. Most of this book was written while we lived together on Enfield Road in Austin, Texas. Nothing would please me more than to annotate each and every single one of these inside jokes, but my editor assigned me a page limit and a "book deadline," so here we are.

Let's take a time machine back to college at Iowa State University in Ames, Iowa. The year was 2007, and I signed a lease with Rachel, Brie, and Katie. This was the start of three years of ugly birthday cakes and hand-me-down decor.

We were weirdos, and we knew it. The first place roommate freedom took us was . . . you guessed it: hair extensions. I don't think any of us thought hair extensions were cool until Brie showed up with full-bodied Sarah Jessica Parker hair (totally kidding—Brie's hair was brown). Brie's bold move gave the rest of us permission to glue strips of fake hair (or was it real hair?) onto our own scalps and save the consequences for later (except for Katie; she never bought in—until Halloween). Were these DIY extensions itchy, nappy, and just the excuse we needed to unapologetically say no to the gym? Absolutely. We looked like mermaids, and we couldn't have been happier. Instead of disposing of them when we were finished (like normal people), we kept them in a bag under our sink, better known as the Bag O'Hair. We weren't sure if we'd need them again for costume parties (Amy Winehouse, Kat Von D) or impromptu rattails, so we made sure to keep them handy.

It's been six years since we shared an Iowa street address, but I still remember because we just had so much *fun*. It was a formative time in life, but we didn't know it because we were too busy going on zombie bar crawls (once), making fun of "Live, Laugh, Love" posters (and all other clichés), borrowing each other's clothes, eating Party Pizzas, and listening to MGMT.

This book is a celebration of roommate life. It is not an account of horror stories or worst-case scenarios; it's an homage to the best of times that have outlived the leases with which they started. It's a reminder to make the most of the moments to come. It's an excuse to celebrate the little things, start dumb traditions, let the hair extensions down, and create space for friendship and play.

Remember, if it's not fun, you're doing it wrong.

Tonight, we lance.

LET'S
DO
THIS

ROOMMATES EXPLAINED

For most of us, roommate life begins at eighteen. We head off to college bright-eyed and bushy-tailed. Dorm living situations are almost always out of our control. Throughout the rest of college and early adult life, roommates are a hodgepodge of strangers, best buds, and friends of friends of cousins' friends.

Just like snowflakes, no two roommates are alike.

ROOMMATE TYPES AS CAFETERIA TABLES

Nobody wants to be put in a box, but since it's easier, we're going to do it anyway. Here is a comprehensive list of roommate types, categorized as if they are cafeteria tables in the 2004 cinema classic *Mean Girls*:

The BFF
'nuff said.

The Random
This is the most common type of roommate. Whether you ended up living together by way of craigslist or the old-fashioned college dorm pairings, all of your life's decisions and experiences have led you to this point. Welcome to the rest of your life.

The Random is like a mysterious one-hundred-acre farm in West Texas. It may always remain desolate and unfamiliar, but if you're lucky, it will make you rich with oil (or memories). Go for the gold and shoot to become best friends by the end of the year.

The "We Get Along but We're Not Really Friends"
I hope you don't kiss your mother with that mouth.

The Braless and Lawless
We all know and love her. She's exposed and she has no filter. She truly embraces her danger zone and has answered the door without pants at least once. She encourages the rest of us to let our hair down and, if nothing else, eat leftover pie for breakfast.

The Frenemy

The Enemy
This was avoidable.

The
BFF

The
Random

The
"We get along
but we're not
really FRIENDS"

The
Braless &
Lawless

The
FRENEMY

The
Enemy

The
"I've never
actually seen
my roommate"

The
Platonic
Opposite Sex

The
Faux
Partner

The "I've Never Actually Seen My Roommate" Roommate

Depending on whom you ask, this is either code for "I'm making the most of it," or "I just won the lottery, nerds."

The Platonic Opposite Sex

Pros: dating advice, somebody to clean the fan blades, probably won't steal your clothes. Cons: shared bathroom (let's not talk about the . . . hair), sports ball posters, can't steal their clothes.

The Faux Partner

One hundred percent platonic, but is more than just a roommate. This is "your person." While similar to the BFF, the faux partner differs in that friends and family regard you as one unit. They know you really are just pals but it's . . . easier this way. It starts by showing up to (all) events together and transitions into FaceTiming each other's families and never ends because one day your future spouses (if you go that route) will invest in a modest commune so nobody ever has to leave.

This is roommate nirvana.

Behind all of these labels are a real bunch of weirdos. I mean, *people.* Weird people just like you and me. Who hasn't been somebody's Random or Braless and Lawless (fingers crossed)?

Maybe you received your first draft pick and landed Phoebe Buffay. *Lucky you.* But for the rest of us—the gang who let craigslist match-make us—these are now our homes filled with beaded curtains and porcelain cat figurines.

Regardless of how we arrived, it is our duty to make the most of this Dougie dance that we call roommate life.

PEACE TREATY

Gratitude is COOL.

Let's start small...

What are three things you're thankful for today?

1. _____
2. _____
3. _____

Now...

What generally _ANNOYS_ you?

What are your expectations?

What will make this YEAR a success?

Hosting badass parties? Keeping a clean house?
Creating memories? Living the crazy stories you will
share with/hide from your grandchildren?

What are the Non-Negotiables?

SHOULD I LIVE WITH THIS PERSON?

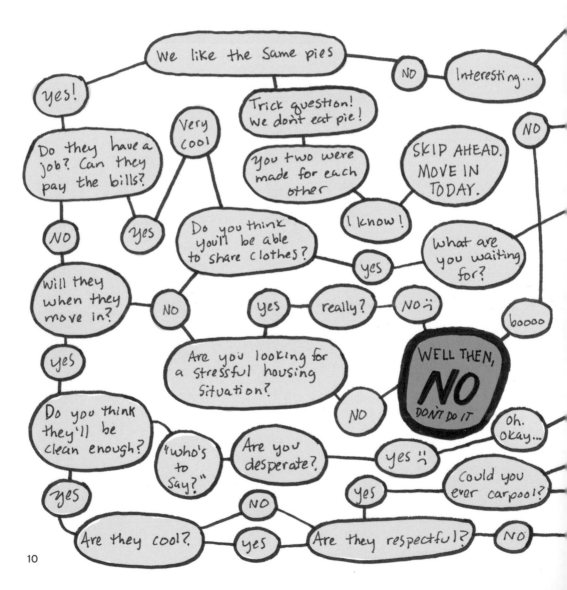

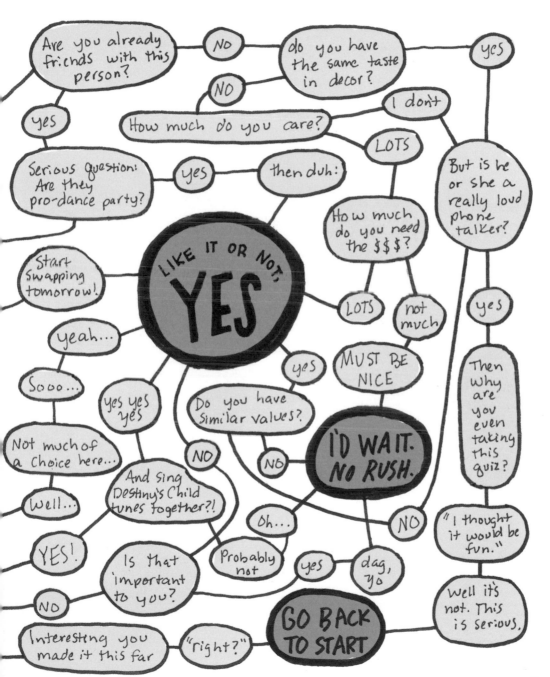

11

3 STEPS to SUCCESS:

1. allow room for faults

2. LIVE in Peace

3. BE thANKful

-Paul

(SomewheRe in Colossians)

MARRIAGE ADVICE FIT FOR ROOMMATES

- ASK QUESTIONS BEFORE OFFERING ADVICE.

- STRIVE TO GIVE MORE THAN YOU RECEIVE.

- DON'T TRY TO CHANGE THEM.

- LET GO OF THE SMALL STUFF.

- DISAGREEMENT IS NOT ALWAYS BAD.

- DO NOT ATTEMPT HOUSE PROJECTS WITHOUT WILLIE NELSON AND A BOWL OF GUAC (SAYS MY FRIEND JENNY AND SHE'S RIGHT).

- STAY CHILL.

DESTINATION SOUL SISTERS

FRESH START

Welcome to the start of a new era. Signing the lease is like signing a (one-year) marriage license. This is the land of opportunity for creating awesome memories. Better yet, these memories come at half price, because hey, that's why you decided to share this four-hundred-square-foot space in the first place. Living with whimsy should start at the moment two or more (roomies) become one (lease).

Should roommates talk about expectations and potential problem areas such as cleanliness, communication, and respect? Sure. But they should also talk about connecting tin can phones to each other's bedrooms and not *if*, but *when*, to host the very first brinner* party.

*Breakfast for dinner.

Top 10 Reasons it's awesome to have a roommate

1. Someone else to kill the spiders

2. Second opinion on thrifted clogs

3. It is impossible to be permanently locked out

4. It takes WAY LESS TIME to fill a load of whites

5. CARPOOLING. Duh.

6. There's always someone
to zip your dress

7. <u>DISPLACE</u> <u>THE</u> <u>BLAME</u>
(eg., messes and bad smells)

8. EVERYTHING is half PRICE

9. Someone is always there to validate
and affirm your every decision

10. Two words:
⁼ SHARING EVERYTHING ⁼

CONVERSATION TOPICS & HYPOTHETICALS

The year is 1900 plus the last two digits of your phone number. You are the same age as you are now. What does your life look like?

Do you remember your last humble brag?
"I always get mascara on my glasses because my eyelashes are so long."
"Every time I fly first class, I end up sitting next to a heavy snorer."

Let's say your car (exactly how it is right now) gets turned into a stretch limousine. How do you stock the refrigerator? Who is the driver? Where is your first trip and whom do you bring?

Would you rather date someone with a rattail or someone with a pencil mustache?

You're trying to break a bad habit. In the name of emotional incentive, you agree to write a check to the organization you most loathe. If you don't fulfill the requirement, they will receive the check. What is this organization?

Would you rather confess an embarrassing habit to every person you meet or do that habit in front of every person you will never see again?

Who would you pick as your TV parents, assuming that they would be exactly as they are on TV and you wouldn't have their kids as siblings?

Who would you pick as your TV siblings given the same qualifications?

What three famous people born on the same day as you would you want to attend your birthday party? (Question may require Internet research.)

Would you rather experience life in fast motion or backward?

If you could have a dinner party with any six people, who would you invite? (They must be alive.)

Would you rather have Justin Bieber give you a ride to school/work every day for a week or have Kanye West give a toast at your graduation/wedding?

Assuming you have to lie about having previously dated somebody semi-famous, what would your semi-believable story be?

What three people that you've met less than three times would you want to be your bandmates?

For reasons the White House cannot disclose, the president and vice president are taking a leave of absence for the next two months. In a fashion similar to jury duty, you are randomly selected to fill in. Do you think you could hold the country together? And if so, what world leader would you first befriend?

You are the organizer of your dream festival. Who are the headlining bands, comedians, and keynote speakers? What is this festival called?

You are a major league baseball player (obviously!). What song (and what part of the song) is played when you step up to the plate?

Who would you want to play you in a movie about yourself?

What is the title of your *New York Times* best-selling memoir?

ROOMMATE UTOPIA

loves pie

loves to bake

Loves to Shop. Loves to Share.

Hates to Shop. Loves to borrow.

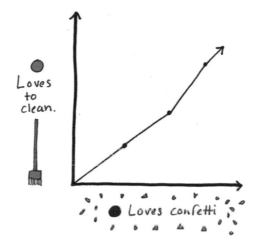

Loves to clean.

Loves confetti

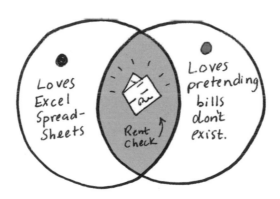

Loves Excel Spread-Sheets

Rent Check

Loves pretending bills don't exist.

● Roommate 1   ● Roommate 2

NICKNAMES

FOR LIFE! / THIS YEAR

—The—
Double Up
Hannah → HanHan

—The—
Play on Words
Drie → Drieyoncé

—The—
Diploma
Master Heather

—The—
Alter Ego
Karen = Courtney Love → Court

—the—
Inner Animal
Sue Dawgg

—The—
Switcheroo
Jen Nickels → Nen Jickels

—The—
Letter Swap
Lindsey → Zindzey

—The—
Signature Trait
Cautious Kathy → CK

—The—
Physical Descriptor
Short Laurel → Lil L

—The—
Pro Wrestler
Molly → The Iron Beast

GOOD ROOMMATE AT A GLANCE →

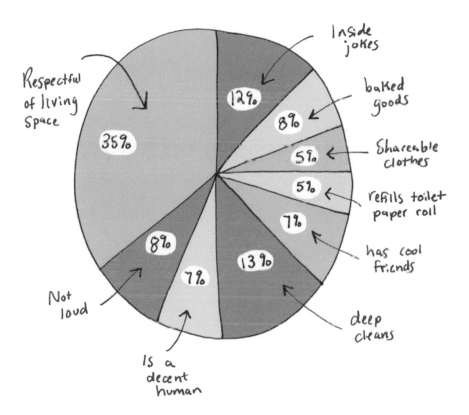

Respectful of living space — 35%

Inside jokes — 12%

baked goods — 8%

Shareable clothes — 5%

refills toilet paper roll — 5%

has cool friends — 7%

deep cleans — 13%

Is a decent human — 7%

Not loud — 8%

No ONE looks STUPID when they're having FUN.

—Amy Poehler

PERSONALITY TYPES
TYPES
REVEALED

Unlike neck tattoos, personality tests are for everyone. Scour the Internet for Enneagram, Myers-Briggs, and DiSC tests. Scour this chapter for the pertinent stuff like:

"What kind of houseplant are you?"

"Are you a 'Handy Han'?"

"What's your indoor pet spirit animal?"

And **"clean freak vs. good enough."**

What kind of houseplant are you?

AIRPLANE PLANT

SAN PEDRO CACTUS

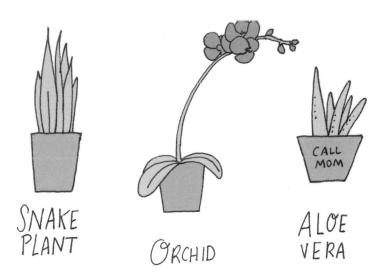

SNAKE
PLANT

ORCHID

CALL
MOM

ALOE
VERA

"Don't you go dyin' on me!"
—Lloyd Christmas

what's your
(INDOOR PET)
SPIRIT ANIMAL?

What statement best describes you?

1. "I'm clean and I prefer my living quarters stay that way. I'd rather be described as adorable than scary, but that doesn't mean I'm soft. Of course by 'soft' I mean a pushover. I am actually quite soft. I enjoy FM radio stations and my favorite season is summer. I also enjoy casual crafting on the weekends."

2. "My messes are contained in my own living space. I do have some *opinions,* and I don't mind who hears them. I have a personality and I'm usually the one to stand out at parties. I think the song 'Billy Jean' by Michael Jackson is overrated, but I see why people like it. I always mark 'unaffiliated' on my voter registration card."

3. "I'm playful and full of energy. Sometimes my curiosity has gotten me into trouble or led me to the wrong place. I like the Beatles, but mostly just the hits that everybody knows. I consider any drive longer than two hours a road trip."

4. "I'm pretty clean; I guess I just don't overthink it. I'm definitely a 'people person.' It's not that I'm type A, it's just that I work well with a schedule. I like to know what to expect. I love people, naps, running, and most rap music."

5. "My favorite hobbies are hanging out, observing sports, and reading. I love reading so much that if there's a movie, I've probably read the book first (sorry about it). I would describe myself as pretty independent, much like most of my favorite films. I prefer to be left alone."

6. "I'm so chill that I just mosey around all day and night thinking about free will and what kind of legacy I want to leave. I also think about the complexity of gentrification and how to foster a climate of diversity in an authentic way. The environment is very important to me."

What did you pick?

See spirit animal on following spread.

1. Chinchilla

2. Bird

3. Ferret

4. Dog

5. Cat

6. Fish
(Sorry, but you did this to yourself.)

ARE YOU A HANDY HAN?

A "Handy Han" is simply a handy woman.
Every home needs one.

Do you qualify? Take this quiz to find out.

Directions: Indicate whether each of the following sixteen statements describes you by marking it "Yes" or "No." At the end, tally up your answers to find out if you are indeed a Handy Han.

1. The Wi-Fi isn't working, but you don't fret because you know how to check the router (or modem?) before calling the cable company.

2. You assemble IKEA furniture on your first try.

3. You can fix* a creaky door.
Spraying cooking oil on the hinge counts.

4. No such thing as a dumpy day with you around . . . because you know how to plunge a toilet.

5. Smoke detector batteries? Too easy.

6. It doesn't matter how you blew the fuse, but you did. Thankfully you know how to reset the power box.

7. You know what a 6-in-1 screwdriver is.

8. You know what day the trash goes out.

9. You broke the toggle of your fan blade. You're short and had to jump to reach it and accidentally pulled it off. Whatever! Why are we still talking about this? You at least have the resourcefulness to Google what to do next.

10. That IKEA bed from statement No. 2 just broke. Do you fix it or just buy a new one? (You lose both ways. No points awarded.)

11. You not only know that the air filter needs to be replaced, but you actually replace it. (Slow clap.)

12. The shower is draining slower than a sloth stuck in molasses during a snowstorm in Iowa. We don't know how the sloth ended up in Des Moines, but the point is that you've already bought the Drano.

13. You know how to load and properly use a caulk gun.

14. You know which YouTube channels provide the best fix-it tutorials. Bonus points for having to watch those tutorials only once.

15. It's time to move out. Thankfully you know how to patch up those seven holes in your kitchen wall when you couldn't find the stud.

16. You can find the stud.

How'd you do?

If you answered thirteen or more statements with an emphatic "Yes!," then you are a Handy Han. If you did not, then your landlord probably hates you.

CLEAN FREAK VS. GOOD ENOUGH

1. Be honest. How often do you wash your sheets?

a. Regularly.
b. When the stains look like Shark Week arrived early.
c. When they reek of my own body odor.

2. Tell us about your floors.

a. They're so clean that I could serve dinner on them . . . but I won't.
b. I sweep at times.
c. Home of fallen hairs, dust bunnies, nail clippings, ice cream drips, and decaying cockroaches.

3. Based on your shower's current level of cleanliness, in what movie would it best belong?

a. *Clueless* (pristine).
b. *Juno* (clean enough).
c. *No Country for Old Men* (Hepatitis, anyone?).

4. What is your method for organizing your Tupperware cabinet?

a. Arranged by shape and size and paired with appropriate lids.
b. In there somewhere.
c. Throw it in, then shut the door as fast as possible.

5. True or False: You consider cleaning out the fridge deep cleaning.

a. False. That is part of "regular cleaning."
b. Depends on when it was last cleaned.
c. TRUE.

6. Somebody is going to swing by abruptly. You have five minutes and your house looks like it does now. How do you proceed?

a. It's fairly clean, but of course I'll still tidy up this and that.
b. Turn down for what? Cleaning, that's what. Time to get to work.
c. They probably won't smell that expired chicken in the trash. . . .

THE RESULTS:

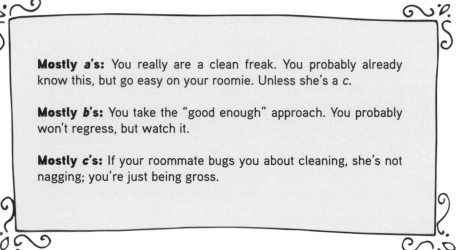

Mostly *a*'s: You really are a clean freak. You probably already know this, but go easy on your roomie. Unless she's a *c*.

Mostly *b*'s: You take the "good enough" approach. You probably won't regress, but watch it.

Mostly *c*'s: If your roommate bugs you about cleaning, she's not nagging; you're just being gross.

49

SHARING LIVES & SLAPPING FIVES

HOSTING AND PARTIES

52

Half the fun of creating your own space is sharing it with others. Learn the trade secrets of receiving five-star hostess ratings without using your nonexistent guest bedroom. Dare to dream! Stand out by making your overnight guests feel extra welcome with a few of these tips and tricks.

While you're at it, impress your local friends by replacing fancy dinner parties with creative get-togethers (food fights and themed parties). Don't forget to provide the MASH (see page 64) and blanket forts. Good things come to those who roommate.

Must-haves
For Overnight Guests

Would you like to win MVP host? Whether it be for your friend's accountant's nephew's girlfriend, who needs a place for the weekend (comic book convention), or your childhood BFF, here's a handy list of supplies. No guest room needed!

Air Mattress

Clean Sheets

Spare Pillow

Clean Towels

For the Overachiever

26-Pound bag of gummy bears

Flowers?

Spare Key

Chocolate

Breakfast

Welcome banner, duh

BUILDING A
CHEESE PLATE

1. Select 3-4 cheeses.
   Contrast texture and taste (soft, semi-hard, hard)

CHEDDAR
CHEESE

GOAT CHEESE

GOUDA

BLUE CHEESE

BRIE

2. Add entourage. Three friends:

Savory :

KALAMATA OLIVES

NUTS

PROSCIUTTO

SALAMI

CRACKERS AND/OR BREAD:

Sweet :

JAM

HONEY

GRAPES

APPLES

3. Let cheese breathe for an hour at room temperature before serving.

4. Do your best to be classy and not inhale all the cheese at once.

HOSTING IDEAS

Game Night • Themed Party • Food Fight • Brinner Party
Movie Marathon • Dance Party • Friendsgiving • Show and Tell
Clothing Swap Party • Slumber Party* • Pumpkin-Carving Contest
Craft Night • Brunch (AKA Breakfestival) • Tea Party • Wine Tasting
Ice Cream Eating Contest • Galentine's Day • Saturday Morning Cartoons

*See "A Case for Blanket Forts" on page 60.

PARTY THEMES

Dress Like the Era of Your Street Address (for example, 4201 = futuristic)
Muumuus and Mimosas • Masquerade • Kentucky Derby
Holiday Party at the Wrong Time of Year
Dress Like Your Favorite Woman from History

COME FOR THE
FROZEN PIZZA
STAY FOR THE
BOARD GAMES

A CASE FOR BLANKET FORTS

Finally! Something for the dinner party–challenged. Problem: You want to host a night of "truth or truth" with your gal pals but you haven't the slightest idea of how to spell gazpacho (sp?), much less make it.

Solution: fort night. Here's why:

1. Hosting becomes easy. Nobody expects you to make dinner or even provide the wine. When folks are in the fort, they just want popcorn, cookies, and M&M's. They're so busy being surprised that you actually built the fort that their expectations have already been surpassed.

2. Slumber parties feel more natural than taking your contacts out after a dust storm. The giggles flow like milk and honey. The conversation turns from "coconut or jojoba oil as a moisturizer" to James Van Der Beek's hair. Jeans are exchanged for jammies and checking social media is replaced with a rousing game of MASH (see page 64).

3. In ten years, which of the following scenarios are you most likely to remember from your jolly old roommate days: a) talking about that one time you got sick from eating three-week-old mac and cheese; b) spending hours in front of the mirror getting ready for another weekend out . . . to the library; c) spending quality time cleaning together every Saturday morning; d) building a cozy blanket fort that stays up one week too long and fifty-one weeks too short.

There are no wrong answers unless you picked *a*, *b*, or *c*.

4. Forts are cheaper than water. These days, "hanging out" seems to be synonymous with "spend all your money on movies, bars, restaurants, and concerts." Sure, we could go on hikes, create lip dub music videos, or look at Beyoncé books at our friend's house, but we usually don't have the foresight to think of that. In *A Million Miles in a Thousand Years,* Donald Miller points out that in movies, people don't do small talk in small places. Friends aren't sitting in coffee shops—they're kayaking or running from volcanoes. *Gilmore Girls* is the exception, not the rule. Make that fort come alive and you'll understand.

5. Fort building is as easy as store-bought pie. Rome wasn't built in a day, but if it was made of blanket forts, it would have been built in an hour.

USEFUL SUPPLIES

Blankets/Sheets

pillows

Chairs

Couch

Clothespins, Safety pins, or paper clamps

weights to keep Sheets in place

Resourcefulness!

NEVER BE
LESS INTERESTING
than YOUR
REfRiGERATOR
MAGNETS.
-DEMETRI MARTIN

MASH REVISITED

Goal: Predict the future. **Instructions:** 1) Fill out the following template with desired answers. 2) Roommate randomly picks a number between one and ten. 3) Roommate uses that number to eliminate answers. For example, if the number is five, roommate starts at the first category and crosses out every fifth answer until there is only one left in each category. 4) Roommate reveals to you your fate. 5) Switch roles.

Boos:

1.
2.
3.
4.

Dream home location:

1.
2.
3.
4.

Exotic pet and name:

1.
2.
3.
4.

Age you receive your first mom haircut:

1.
2.
3.
4.

Your cause:

1.
2.
3.
4.

If you went back to college, you'd study:

1.
2.
3.
4.

thing you do
once a year:

1.

2.

3.

4.

your famous
grandchild will
be known for:

1.

2.

3.

4.

Tax Bracket:

1.

2.

3.

4.

where you
will retire:

1.

2.

3.

4.

Mortgage:

1.

2.

3.

4.

Regrettable
fashion choice:

1.

2.

3.

4.

Proudest moment:

1.

2.

3.

4.

firstborn's name:

1.

2.

3.

4.

You shared a cab
with this celebrity:

1.

2.

3.

4.

STAY IN VS. GO OUT

Staying IN

- FORT
- home made cookies
- (CHEAP) WINE
- WRITE PREdictioNs
- MAKE Time CapSule
- MASH reVisited
- PictuRes + Videos
- tell SecRets
- No bRas

GOINg Out

- Have a chance to lower cost per wear on new shoes
- lipstick
- See MoRe folks

"ONE OF MY NEW YEAR'S RESOLUTIONS is to say 'YES!' YES to LOVE, YES to LIFE, YES TO STAYING IN MORE!"

—LIZ LEMON

STARTING TRADITIONS

Don't wait for permission (or mom jeans) to start implementing traditions. Whether they're silly or serious, they're what we remember long after the lease is up.

Be proactive, seek whimsy, and delight in the unusual.

Godspeed!

WHY TRADITIONS?

TRADITIONS NOW: INSIDE JOKES LATER

BYOST

(BUILD YOUR OWN SET OF TRADITIONS)

After big accomplishments, we _____.

Every time _____, we _____.

On the first of the month, we _____.

On birthday mornings, we _____.

Whenever we finish a project, we _____.

rewatch favorite movie • sleep in
record a new music video • get pedicures
eat a whole pie • go out for ice cream
visit a nursing home • buy flowers
bake more cookies for the mailman
make signature drink • explore a new part of town
call the fam • bake zucchini muffins

MORE FREE IDEAS:

SPECIFIC GIFTS FOR SPECIFIC ACHIEVEMENTS

"SPECIAL PLATE"

MUG FOR EVERY MARATHON... RIDICULOUS

THE ONE-OFF PLATE FOR SPECIAL OCCASIONS

DESIGNATED SONG FOR A DESIGNATED DANCE BREAK

KARAOKE FT. YOUR GO-TO DUET

"...cuz I want it all... or nothing at all..."

DECORATE ROOMMATE'S PARKING SPOT WITH SIDEWALK CHALK

SECRET HANDSHAKES

FRIDAY NIGHT PIZZA

MONDAY MORNING MIMOSAS

MAKE EACH OTHER'S BIRTHDAY CAKES

HB, OR WHATEVER

WEEKLY TV SHOW

IF IT'S NOT FUN, YOU'RE DOING IT WRONG.

CRAFTING FOR TWO

Sick and tired of posting another project to your Pinterest DIY board all the while knowing you are never going to make that floral antler necklace display? How about the doily table runner? Did you really think you'd learn how to sew just to turn your old jeans into a messenger bag?

Crafting is an easy and cheap way to spruce up the home and spruce up your life! The following pages are filled with house projects that will cost you no more than a good cocktail.

13 WAYS TO PAINT YOUR TERRA-COTTA POT

What do you call a naked succulent? A plant without a pot. Fetch yourself a terra-cotta pot, small paint brush, white paint (or glitter!), and a commercial break. The possibilities are endless, but here are a few to get you started.

Note: These also make great housewarming gifts.

your roommate's portrait

some pattern that's impossible to mess up

plant's name

a reminder

something understated

eyes, because they're so hot right now

beard stubble/"stars"
(a bunch of dots)

a great haircut

581-8

your SSN (JK)

Flowers or
whatever

yourmother
↑
all
lowercase

your Wi-Fi password,
so you can point to it
like a disgruntled barista
when guests ask.

LESS
BUT
BETTER

your
mantra

Why?
How could
what els

Socratic
questions

What are the consequences
of that assumption?

Time Capsule

here's what you need:

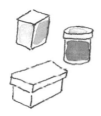

CONTAINER

PAPER

Pen!

OBJECT YOU CAN LIVE WITHOUT

MEMORIES

hiding PLACE

LIST OF QUESTIONS

DIY FIREPLACE

Supplies needed:
- giant sheet of paper
- markers
- drawing skills

TIN CAN TELEPHONES

TO CONNECT TO BEDROOMS!

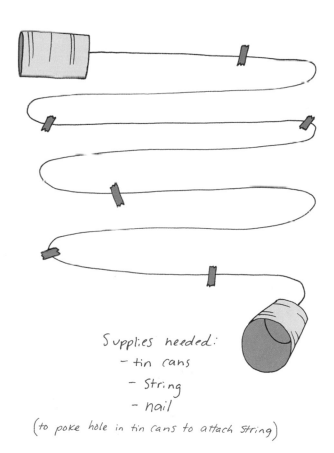

Supplies needed:
- tin cans
- string
- nail

(to poke hole in tin cans to attach string)

POOR WOMAN'S GUIDE TO DECORATING

1. Sunday estate sales (usually 1/2 price).
2. When in doubt, spray paint it gold.
3. Subscribe to minimalism.
4. Always accept hand-me-downs.

PRANKTOWN, USA

What else is a craft? **Pranking.**

Well, it's really more of an art.

Remember, to the degree that you prank, you, too, shall be pranked. (Consider this when contemplating the slumber party one-eyebrow shave.) All pranks are in good humor and nothing of permanence . . . except the memories!

A few ideas:

1. Confetti on the fan blade.

2. Flour in the blow dryer.

3. Move everything in roommate's bedroom over an inch each day and see how long it takes them to notice.

4. Replace Oreo frosting with toothpaste.

5. Prankster 101: Pour a glass of ice cold water over the shower curtain while roommate is showering. *Or* just dump a glass of ice cold water over her anytime, anywhere.

Be prepared for immediate repercussions.

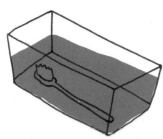

Jello toothbrush
★★

Put clear nail polish
on their bar of soap.
★

Fill deodorant
with cream cheese.
★

LEVEL OF EFFORT:

★ Easy Peasy   ★★ Requires planning

COMFORT CITY

$PLITTING BILLS AND SHARING CLOTHES

What do periods, clothes, and cleaning supplies all have in common? They're meant to be shared by you and your roommate. As discussed, one of the best reasons to have a roommate is the ability to borrow (or lend) just about everything.

That means twice as many kitchen gadgets, books, and nail polish colors at half the price. But don't stop there. Share ideas, food (with permission), friends, furniture, and household chores.

I don't have high expectations or anything, But Feel Free to Share the following:

1. Your artisan focaccia bread that you purchased against your better judgment after you said that no bread is $8 good.

2. Your funny stories and mannerisms, but I will agree to use them only in the presence of those whom you will never meet.

3. Your mother's Netflix username and password.

4. Your face wash, toothpaste, almond milk, peanut butter, and flax seeds on the occasion that I run out of my own all of a sudden and haven't the willpower to go to the local grocer.

5. Your rare vintage stamp collection under your bed.

6. Your party pants (leggings).

7. A slice of leftover cake from dinner with your family for your brother's graduation.

8. Your bobby pins, hair ties (did I mention soap?), hairspray, and all other necessary but unimportant trifles.

9. Your downtown parking pass.

10. Your Essie nail polish in select colors: Madison Ave-Hue, Hide and Go Chic, Truth or Flare, Ignite the Night, and For the Twill of It.

11. Your company (as my driver) on nights we go out and I happen to be out of gas or my taillight needs replaced.

12. Your infinity scarf, but only when you are out of town.

13. Your listening ears if you ever want to help me dissect a perplexing text message or help justify why I eat what I eat. I invite you to sit back, enjoy a glass of your almond milk, and help me debrief.

14. Your feedback on my color blocking, pattern mixing, and all other fashion woes.

15. Your Burgundy Wine lipstick.

16. Your full-length mirror.

17. Your antique ring. You know, the one your aunt gave you that belonged to your grandmother. The one where the stone is from her princess friend in British Guiana. I'd only wear it for special occasions (New Year's and first dates).

18. There's more! ⟶

19. Your high standards for yourself and others.

20. Your vintage Pentax 35 mm camera. I won't use any of the film; I just want it displayed on my shelf.

21. Your wide-tooth shower comb, because, honestly, we don't need two of those.

22. Your ironic Looney Tunes jersey.

23. Your parents' old record player. The one with a blown-out speaker, but plays the new Bastille record better than any live concert.

24. One of the flowers from your birthday bouquet from your boyfriend. I just want to put it in my tiny vase by my nightstand (or on my desk).

25. Your dry shampoo.

26. Your taste in obscure foreign flicks. Fear not, I will never actually watch them. I will only name-drop as I see fit.

You can either Practice being Right or practice being KIND.

—ANNE LAMOTT

Things you can share

Necklaces

Hats

Condiments

furniture

Friends

ideas and conversation

EXPERT LEVEL:

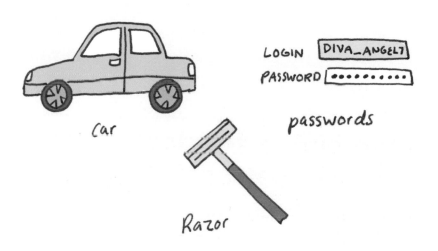

car

LOGIN DIVA_ANGEL7
PASSWORD ●●●●●●●●●●

passwords

Razor

Things you probably shouldn't share:

Boyfriends

BEST-CASE SCENARIOS:

A: "I ate the rest of your pizza. I'm the worst."

B: "That's okay! I'm just glad it didn't go to waste."

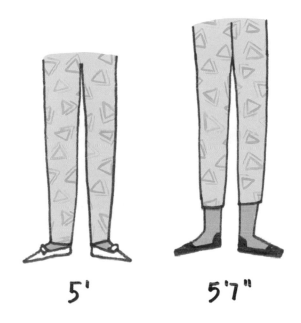

5'   5'7"

SAME PANTS

COCKROACH is here

Cover unwanted pests with cup until roommate returns. Hopefully she will have the courage to properly exterminate.

Should I eat that without asking?

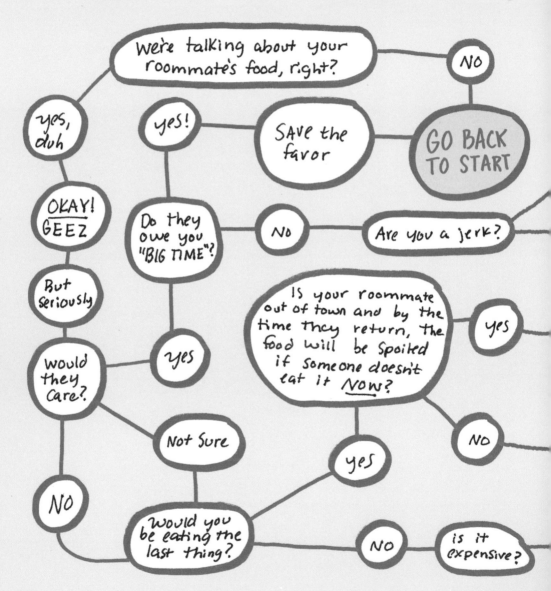

STAGES of Comfort

1.
Bedroom
isolation

2.
Opens door
to say hi
to cat.

3.
Willing to
share bathroom

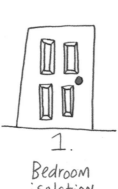

4.
Never closes
bathroom door

5.
Never
wears pants

6.
Answers door
without pants

EISENHOWER MATRIX (FOR CHORES!)

Just how did our thirty-fourth president get **so much*** done?
He prioritized.

"What is important is seldom urgent and what is urgent is seldom important."
– Dwight D. Eisenhower

One of his famous methods for productivity is known as the Eisenhower Matrix. In it, he categorizes tasks into one of four parts:

important , urgent , not important , not urgent

This can be used for all sorts of things (like getting your life together) but let's just warm up with house chores.

After checking out this -VERY- helpful example,
go ahead and make your own. Sally forth!

*Five-star army general, supreme commander of Allied forces in Europe during WWII, served two terms as president, started programs that led to the interstate highway system, the Internet, and space exploration.

Example:

URGENT   NOT URGENT

IMPORTANT

- Wash yoga pants
- take out trash
- Straighten up house like a decent human
- put away groceries

- Change smoke detector batteries
- deep clean bathroom
- dust
- wash sheets

1 | **2**

3 | **4**

NOT IMPORTANT

- Film "Wrecking Ball" parody with balancing ball while music video is still fairly relevant. *NOT A CHORE
- be first to prank roomie

- Rearrange furniture
- Organize bookshelf (LOL)
- Tidy up best nook for "impromptu" Instagram. # home # blessed

MAKE FRIENDSHIP NOT WAR

Perhaps your roommate always eats your tortillas, or maybe she never refills the ice cube tray. Either way, it just. pisses. you. off.

Remember to pick your battles.

But before you pick the battle, don't forget about the time you were running late to water aerobics and left the kitchen in shambles. Or the time you invited your singing improv troupe over unannounced while your roommate was trying to film her audition tape for *The Amazing Race*.

We're all in this together.

CONFRONTATION

Sometimes roommate confrontation can be tough.

"Hey, could you pay me back this week for your half of our 'GO AWAY' welcome mat?"

Sometimes we don't even ask for it, but just by existing, we're thrown into the lion's den (à la honest feedback).

"Is this black bra under my sheer white knit top noticeable? I already wore it to an interview."

Sometimes we have to stand up for ourselves.

"Please stop calling yourself brunette. I know you think you dyed your hair brown, but you're still very blond, comparatively."

"When you put the empty peanut butter jar in the cupboard it makes me feel *sad* because I think there will be peanut butter, but there *isn't*."

Honesty is nice.

It's essential for real relationships.

With honesty comes what is arguably the most confrontational thirteen-letter word in the English language: confrontation.

But it's good for us.

Be sincere and be kind.

Now let's put the "fun" back in confuntation, and remember:

"Be the thoughtful roommate you want to see refilling the toilet paper roll in the apartment." —Mother Teresa

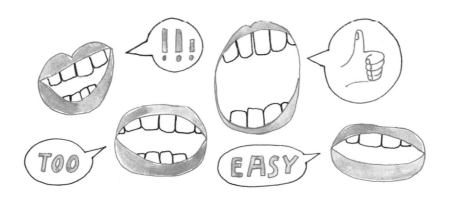

TRUE FRIENDS
STAB YOU IN
THE FRONT.
— OSCAR WILDE

PET PEEVE AWARENESS

*NOTE HOW THESE ALL HAVE TO DO WITH CLEANLINESS

NOT REPLACING THE TOILET PAPER

EMPTY CONTAINERS

TOOTHPASTE IN SINK

DIRTY COUNTER

NOT REFILLING THE ICE CUBE TRAYS

HAIR IN SINK

"My name is_____
and I wash all the dishes."

HOW TO LOSE A ROOMMATE IN TEN MONTHS

1. Unapologetically steal all the tampons.

2. Don't clean up your nail clippings.

3. Potty train pets to use toilet.

4. Refuse to pay for common household items because you don't "use them."

5. Cook fish, don't wash dishes, repeat.

6. talk loudly.

7. Chew loudly.

8. Breathe loudly.

9. Spend collected rent money on souped-up Vespa.

10. Purposely lock your roommate out because, you know, privacy.

It's Okay
to be
different.

Likes the temperature at 72°F.

Likes the temperature at 67°F.

A little gratitude
goes a long way.

Thank you for all the times you've cleaned the bathroom after I said I really would this week :/

Thank you for letting me move the space heater around with me wherever I go in the apartment. (This is why I call it the "adult blankie.")

Thank you for understanding when I said I didn't like your "live, laugh, love" poster.

Thank you for letting me debrief every night, no matter how late, after that string of awkward & dates.

Thank you for telling me it was him that made it weird, not me.

and if nothing else, thank you for that culotte pant intervention.

xo,
B

Thank you for not getting mad when I told you I accidentally use your toothbrush sometimes.

¯_(ツ)_/¯

Thank you for wearing my clothes because it affirms that I have good style.

REMEMBER...

IF YOU *have*
TERRIBLE
luck with
R°OMMATES,
YOU'RE THE
Terrible
roommate.

—Sarah Silverman

THE YEAR OF ACES

Just like nap time in kindergarten, when roommate life is over, it's over. This season probably won't last forever, so make the most of it. Bake cookies, go on road trips, wear wigs out on the town, buy disposable cameras, and treat your roommate to flowers every now and then just for the heck of it.

Be gracious, give a little more than you take, and seize the day.

There's always something to celebrate.

In second grade I scoffed at the whippersnappers who didn't know how good they had it. While they were counting fives, I was reading Goosebumps and heading for another animal cracker bender.

At eight years old I realized nap time was gone forever. And I missed it.

This is where we are today.

So many of us live like we're in transition. We're not sure what to call this foggy time between leaving the nest and going to college and "maybe start a family . . . JK . . . but if I do, when?" because we still use mismatching sheets and count baking frozen pizza as cooking dinner. We take six a.m. flights because they're $30 cheaper and we still call Mom to ask how to remove gum from our pants (right?). We don't spring for the guacamole because, yes, we know it costs extra and, no, we do not want to pay for it.

And then it happens. We (gasp!) "grow up." We get the relationship, house, dare I say scuba certification, baby, or herb garden. They're here to stay. This is good!

But now we have to shave our legs, get excited about dishwasher warranties, and decide between cloth and regular diapers for our hipster babies.

The next big things are good, and they should be celebrated.

But they shouldn't overshadow the importance of eating nachos for breakfast or hanging a giant drawing of a fireplace in lieu of a real one because your college apartment is not a log cabin, but I digress. You do you.

We must cherish these days.

As in, today's day.

Because like kindergarten nap time, when it's over, it's over.

STAY HERE AS LONG AS YOU CAN.

—BILLY MADISON

I Love to See a young girl go out And grab the WORLd By the Lapels.

— Maya Angelou

BUCKET LIST

 Host a themed party

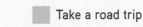 Take a road trip

 Buy roommate flowers

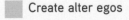 Pizza bomb neighbor

Create alter egos

☐ Wear wigs out

☐ Build a blanket fort

☐ Create a scavenger hunt

☐ Work out together

☐ Make friendship bracelets

☐ Get manicures

☐ Make a lip dub music video

☐ Volunteer together

☐ Make May Day baskets

☐ Give home a nickname

☐ Bonus: create logo for the home

☐ Write thank-you letters

☐ Start a book club

☐ Host an ice cream eating contest

☐ Learn to make a signature drink

Buy a disposable camera

Dress the same in public

Prank each other

Get real (or fake) tattoos

Paint faces for a football game

Take a class together (cooking, ceramics, dance, yoga, etc.)

Order late-night takeout

Bake cookies for mailman

Host a craft night

Get bangs!

Send shared holiday cards

Buy a plant and see how long you can keep it alive

Get piercings!

Go streaking

SIGNATURE POSES

Back-2-Back   Sorority Squat

The Mary-Kate and Ashley

The Party Trick

Fake Laughter

ROOMMATE Gift Ideas

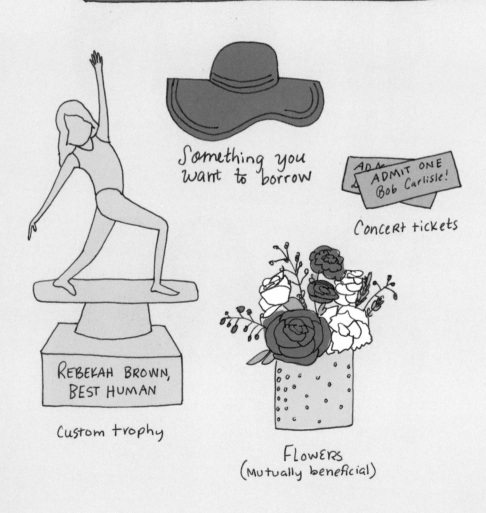

Something you want to borrow

ADMIT ONE
Bob Carlisle!

Concert tickets

REBEKAH BROWN, BEST HUMAN

Custom trophy

FLOWERS
(Mutually beneficial)

Gift card for
nails or massage

FANCY coffee
or tea

Candles

Something she
hates, because
it would
be funny.

(Free Willy 1 + 2
VHS in this case)

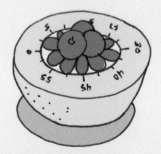

A grapefruit
timer, because
you never know

If all goes
according
to plan...

ACKNOWLEDGMENTS

The timeline of creating this book directly coincides with the relationship with my husband. I had the idea to start this project two weeks before we went on our first date, and now I'm finishing it just a few months after we got married. It feels like I'm saying good-bye to the roommate season while saying hello to a new one. Greg, thank you for supporting me from the moment this was just some idea to now, as I type the final page as your wife. I love you, and I'm glad we're roommates forever.

It wouldn't be possible for me to write a book about roommates if it weren't for all of the weird, wonderful, funny women I lived with for the last eight years. Whether we shared an address for several years or just several months, you are the reason this book exists. Thank you. Specifically, in order of most recent:

Austin, Texas: Rebekah Brown

Waco, Texas: Kelsey and A. J. Henry, Claire (Kultgen) McDonald

Norwalk, Iowa: Cousin Terrell and his wife, Laura, Murphy (and Nolan, Mallory, and Miranda)

Rome, Italy: Karen Mechler, Laura Weible, Leah Hanus, Caroline (Egan) Nicks, Bridget (Miller) Black, and Bethany (Weber) Hepler

Ames, Iowa: Brie (Nickels) Rundall, Rachel (Soe) Kocak, Katie Sheluga, and Stacey Brockett

I also want to give a giant thank-you to my agent, Laurie Abkemeier, and my editor, Patty Rice, who trusted my wacky ideas and put no bounds on my creative freedom.

I have other pals who walked through this with me (and provided helpful edits): Chad Conine, Beth Nervig, Jen Moulton, and a handful of other friends who contributed thoughtful feedback. Big thanks to the Adobe team for supporting me during this Creative Residency so I could fully dive into my passion projects and grow as an artist.

I wouldn't have the nerve to be writing books if it weren't for my supportive parents who would probably be just as impressed if this book was a coaster made of popsicle sticks. Thank you, Mom and Dad. And thank you to the rest of my family: Ryan, Candice, little Kellen, Baby M, Brock, Laurel, and my sweet in-laws, Karen, Steve, Michele, Jamie, John, little Noelle, tiny Ben, Scott, Jackson, and Mason. I'm motivated to make you all proud.

And finally, shout-out to the inside jokes that didn't make the book: Blue Shirts Black Pants What's Up, The Cockroach That Got Away, Pillowman Pranks, "If Danny doesn't win, I'll die!," Bekki the Dinosaur, Italian Disco with Italian Neighbors, The Girls and Kenneth, Pink Guy, "Don't Mountain If I Dewski," Sleeping by the Dumpsters in Cinque Terre, Beckfest Breakfast and College Breakfestivals, Don't Take the Girl (Halloween), "Seven studs in the kitchen wall is good enough," Fallapalooza, helmets during the thunderstorm, and that one time I got stuck in my own driveway and Claire had to build a ramp to bail me out.

Andrews McMeel Publishing
a division of Andrews McMeel Universal
1130 Walnut Street, Kansas City, Missouri 64106

www.andrewsmcmeel.com

16 17 18 19 20 SDB 10 9 8 7 6 5 4 3 2 1

ISBN: 978-1-4494-7090-6

Library of Congress Control Number: 2016930180

Editor: Patty Rice
Art Director: Holly Ogden
Designer: Becky Simpson
Production Manager: Tamara Haus
Production Editor: Erika Kuster

ATTENTION: SCHOOLS AND BUSINESSES
Andrews McMeel books are available at quantity discounts with bulk purchase for educational, business, or sales promotional use. For information, please e-mail the Andrews McMeel Publishing Special Sales Department: specialsales@amuniversal.com.